North American
INDIAN NATIONS

NATIVE PEOPLES
of the
NORTHWEST

Krystyna Poray Goddu

LERNER PUBLICATIONS ◆ MINNEAPOLIS

The editors would like to note that we have made every effort to work with consultants from various nations, as well as fact-checkers, to ensure that the content in this series is accurate and appropriate. In addition to this title, we encourage readers to seek out content produced by the nations themselves online and in print.

Consultant: Jill Campbell, Coordinator, Language and Culture Department (Musqueam First Nation)

Lerner Publications Company
A division of Lerner Publishing Group, Inc.
241 First Avenue North
Minneapolis, MN 55401 USA

For reading levels and more information, look up this title at www.lernerbooks.com.

Main body text set in Rockwell Std Light 12/16.
Typeface provided by Monotype Typography.

Library of Congress Cataloging-in-Publication Data

Names: Goddu, Krystyna Poray, author.
Title: Native peoples of the Northwest / Krystyna Poray Goddu.
Description: Minneapolis : Lerner Publications, [2016] | Series: North American Indian
    nations | Includes bibliographical references and index. | Audience: Ages 8–11.
Identifiers: LCCN 2015047489 (print) | LCCN 2015047590 (ebook) | ISBN 9781467779395
    (lb : alk. paper) | ISBN 9781512412451 (pb : alk. paper) | ISBN 9781512410785 (eb pdf)
Subjects: LCSH: Indians of North America—Northwest, Pacific—Juvenile literature. |
    Northwest, Pacific—Juvenile literature.
Classification: LCC E78.N77 G61 2017 (print) | LCC E78.N77 (ebook) | DDC 979.5004/97-
    -dc23
LC record available at http://lccn.loc.gov/2015047489

Manufactured in the United States of America
1-37532-18675-3/28/2016

CONTENTS

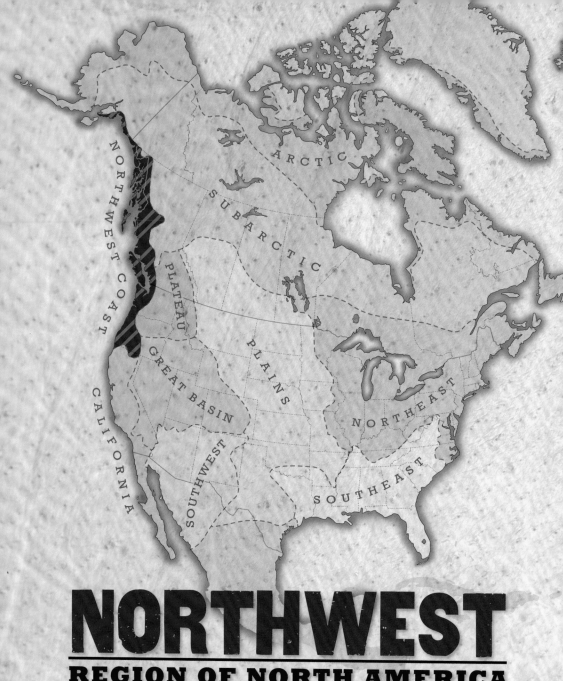

ARCTIC

SUBARCTIC

NORTHWEST COAST

PLATEAU

PLAINS

GREAT BASIN

CALIFORNIA

NORTHEAST

SOUTHWEST

SOUTHEAST

NORTHWEST

REGION OF NORTH AMERICA

CULTURAL REGIONS OF THE UNITED STATES AND CANADA

- Plateau
- Northwest Coast
- California
- Plains
- Southeast
- Southwest
- Great Basin
- Northeast
- Subarctic
- Arctic
- Other

- - - - Cultural area border
———— International border
·········· State/province border

INTRODUCTION

Raven was lonely. He flew over the ocean and landed on the sand. He looked all around him. He didn't see life anywhere. Suddenly he heard strange noises. He discovered a large clamshell in the sand. Inside, Raven saw some tiny, strange-looking creatures. They didn't have fur or feathers like him. They looked scared, and they made noises Raven could not understand.

But Raven was excited to have some company. He wanted to help these creatures. Raven bent down and spoke to them. He wondered how they could survive. He asked them to come out of the shell. It took a long time, but slowly they began to come out. These were the first humans. They were the Haida (HIGH-duh).

The Haida are one of many groups of native peoples living in the Northwest. The region is a thin strip of land and islands along the Pacific coast from Alaska to Northern California. It is only 150 miles (240 kilometers) wide. It covers parts of what are now Alaska, British Columbia, Washington, Oregon, and California. The Pacific Ocean is to the west. The Coast Range and Cascade Range are to the east. This region gets a lot of rain and has mild temperatures.

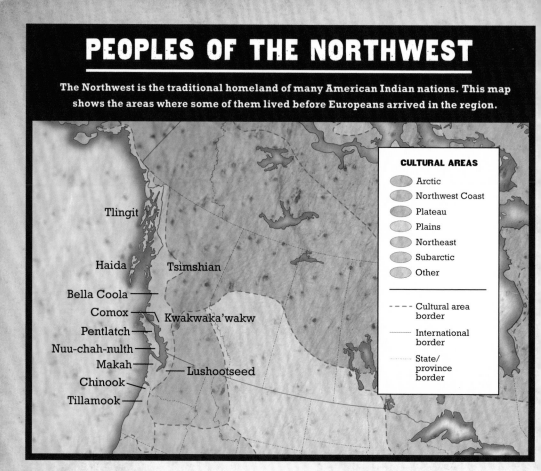

PEOPLES OF THE NORTHWEST

The Northwest is the traditional homeland of many American Indian nations. This map shows the areas where some of them lived before Europeans arrived in the region.

Tlingit

Haida

Tsimshian

Bella Coola

Comox

Kwakwaka'wakw

Pentlatch

Nuu-chah-nulth

Makah

Lushootseed

Chinook

Tillamook

CULTURAL AREAS

Arctic
Northwest Coast
Plateau
Plains
Northeast
Subarctic
Other

- - - - Cultural area border

International border

State/ province border

More than thirty nations lived in this region. They spoke many different languages from different language families. These language families are called Wakashan (wah-KA-shehn), Coast Salish (SAY-lish), Chinook (shi-NOOK), and Tsimshian (CHIM-shee-un). Some nations spoke languages that no other nations spoke. These languages were Tlingit (KLINK-it or TLING-kit) and Haida. Among the better-known Northwest nations are the Tlingit, Haida, Tsimshian, Kwakwaka'wakw (KWAK-walk-ya-walk), Nuu-chah-nulth (NEW-chah-nulth), Makah (mah-KAW), and Chinook. Coast Salish is a language family. But the term is often used to describe the many nations that spoke Coast Salish languages. The Coast Salish region is broken up into North Coast Salish, which includes the Bella Coola (beh-la-KOO-la) nation; Central Coast Salish, which includes the Comox (KOH-muhks), Pentlatch (PENT-latch), and Lushootseed (LUH-shoot-seed); and South Coast Salish, which includes the Tillamook (TILL-ah-muhk). In the United States, these peoples are known as American Indians or Northwest Indians. But in Canada, these nations are referred to as indigenous, aboriginal, or First Nations peoples.

The region is filled with lakes, rivers, and trees. The landscape and weather allow for abundant resources. So the

MEANING OF NATIONS' NAMES

NATION	MEANING
Makah	Cape dwellers
Nuu-chah-nulth	Among the mountains
Tlingit	People
Tsimshian	People inside the Skeena River

The rocky and tree-lined Northwest Coast provided all the resources Northwest Indians needed to thrive in the region.

Northwest Indians never had to worry about finding enough food. This allowed them to spend more time on social and cultural activities. Northwest Indians created and decorated practical items such as dishes and clothing. They practiced many rituals and ceremonies. Their society was broken up into social classes. And due to trade and contact with the Europeans, Northwest Indians were quite wealthy.

Like most American Indians, the nations of the Northwest were forced onto reservations in the nineteenth century. In Canada, the government took away First Nations lands. The nations were left with portions of land called reserves. But the native peoples of the Northwest fought against the loss of their land and traditions. In the twentieth century, the Northwest Indians were able to gain back much of their land and rights. Many Northwest Indians still live on and care for the same lands where their ancestors thrived.

LANGUAGE FAMILIES OF THE NORTHWEST

LANGUAGE FAMILY	MAJOR PEOPLES
Coast Salish	Bella Coola; Comox, Lushootseed, Pentlatch; Tillamook
Tsimshian	Tsimshian
Wakashan	Kwakwaka'wakw, Makah, Nuu-chah-nulth
Tlingit	Tlingit
Haida	Haida
Chinook	Chinook

CHAPTER 1

AN ABUNDANT LAND

The Pacific Northwest is filled with streams and forests. The Northwest Indians had many food sources. There was lots of wood too. Cedar was used for everything from building homes and canoes to weaving clothing and carving tools.

Canoes like this one were important for trade, travel, and fishing in the Northwest.

The Haida used large hooks like this one carved of wood to catch halibut.

Food

The sea and rivers were full of fish, including salmon, halibut, candlefish, and shellfish. The most important seafood was salmon. Many Northwest peoples trapped salmon every spring. They usually smoked the fish over a fire. Then they used candlefish oil to preserve the salmon until the next year.

The Haida fished for halibut from Haida Gwaii, also called the Queen Charlotte Islands. Halibut swim along the bottom of the ocean. They sometimes weigh up to 400 pounds (180 kilograms). To catch them, the Haida dropped large V-shaped hooks deep into the water. When they caught a fish, they had to work quickly to make sure the giant struggling fish did not flip the canoe.

The Northwest Indians also caught whales, seals, and porpoises. To catch these large animals, the Northwest Indians traveled in huge dugout canoes. The canoes were made from the trunks of giant cedar trees. They might be decorated with carvings. Northwest Indians used smaller canoes too. Rocky cliffs lined the coast. So traveling by canoe was easier and faster than traveling by land.

Along with fishing, men also hunted deer, elk, mountain goats, and bears. Women gathered plant bulbs, roots, berries,

SALMON

Salmon were very important to the Northwest Indians. Many Northwest nations tell the legend of the salmon people who lived all winter beneath the ocean. Every spring, the salmon people changed into fish and swam upriver. There, the Northwest Indians caught and ate them. When the salmon people turned into fish, their human souls went into the ocean. If their bones or insides were put back into the water, the salmon people could come back to life. The next spring they would be able to swim upriver again. In this way, the salmon people sacrificed themselves for the Northwest Indians each spring.

The Northwest Indians honored the salmon with the first-salmon ceremony. The first salmon caught each spring was sprinkled with eagle feathers or a powdery, colored clay called ocher. The people thanked and welcomed the salmon. Then the fish was cooked and cut into tiny pieces. The pieces were fed to everybody at the ceremony. The bones were thrown back into the sea. Almost every Northwest nation practiced the first-salmon ceremony.

and seeds. They made cakes from pressed sea plants too. The Northwest Indians had a rich and varied diet.

Homes

Most Northwest Indians built their homes on the sand or gravel beaches near the water. They usually used cedar to build large rectangular houses. These were often called plank houses. Several related families lived together in the same house.

To build their homes, the Northwest Indians created a frame of logs. They then attached wide wooden planks to the logs. The roof and floor were also made from planks. The houses could be anywhere from 20 feet (6 meters) wide and 30 feet (9 m) long to as large as 60 feet (18 m) wide and 100

A traditional Chinook cedar plank house

THE OZETTE MUDSLIDE

Between three hundred and five hundred years ago, a mudslide covered the Makah whaling village of Ozette, in Washington. When the village was discovered, archaeologists found well-preserved skeletons, houses, furniture, and items such as baskets and fishing tools. From these artifacts they were able to learn a lot about the Makah Nation and their whaling culture. Many of these discoveries are on display at the Makah Museum in the Makah Cultural and Research Center at Neah Bay, Washington, on the Makah Reservation.

feet (30 m) long. Inside, there were platforms for sleeping and storage along the walls. In the middle was a fire pit. A hole in the roof above it let the smoke out. Cedar mats hung from the low ceilings to create separate spaces for families.

These plank homes were permanent homes for the Northwest Indians. But for hunting, gathering, and fishing, the people would break into groups and leave the village. These groups would travel in search of food. They usually went to camps where they knew they could find resources.

Villages were made up of several plank houses. These houses were built in a row, and they all faced the water. The front of the house was often painted. A village chief or the head of a family assigned living spaces to each family. When the head of the family died, the house would be given away or burned down. The family moved to another house so that the spirit of the person who had died would not be bothered.

Clothing

In the summer, men often did not wear clothes. In the winter, they wore knee-length tunics made from woven cedar bark and rabbit fur. Women wore aprons of woven cedar bark. They also wore skirts. Tsimshian and Haida women made their skirts of bark. Tlingit women wore skirts made of deerskin. The Chinook used shredded or split cedar fibers to make their skirts. Sometimes women wore tunics like the men.

Fur robes made of sea otter, seal, bear, raccoon, and bobcat fur were popular among the Northwest nations. Coast Salish peoples wove robes from the wool of mountain goats. After Europeans came to the area, Northwest Indians began

Bark from cedar trees was used to weave clothing items such as tunics, aprons, and skirts.

Northwest nations used Hudson's Bay blankets like this one to make coats. These blankets continue to be very popular.

trading for clothing. Woolen blankets made in England and sold by the Hudson's Bay Company were especially valued. Northwest peoples used these blankets to make coats.

Northwest Indians usually did not wear shoes. In the winter, they sometimes wore moccasins or snowshoes. The snowshoes were made from wood that was steamed or soaked until it was soft enough to bend. Thin strips of deerskin were used as lacing.

Both men and women wore necklaces made from shells, animal teeth, antlers, bones, or thin copper beads. They also pierced their noses and ears. The Tlingit and Haida pierced the lips of young girls. As the girls grew up, they wore a piercing called a labret in their lips. The labrets were made of small oval pieces of shell, wood, ivory, or bone.

Men wore their hair in a bun on top of their heads or long and loose. Many of them had goatees or mustaches. Women usually wore their hair in braids. Sometimes they put carved wood or shell pendants into the braids.

Face painting was common among the Northwest Indians. The paint protected their skin from the sun and wind. They used black, white, and red paint made from roots, berries, clay, and tree bark. Northwest Indians painted their faces for ceremonies too.

A Tlingit woman dressed in ceremonial clothing, including a beaded chest plate and a bear claw hat

Tattooing was another tradition. Men might have tattoos on the chest, back, arms, and legs. Women wore tattoos on the chest, shoulders, arms, hands, and lower legs. The tattoos were often a sign of status. They might show a spiritual figure or a family crest. Some tattoo designs were passed down through families.

CHAPTER 2

FAMILY AND
SPIRITUAL LIFE

Northwest Indian society was made up of three classes of people. Among the Tlingit, the highest-ranking people were known as the *taises*. They came from the wealthiest families. Below them were the ordinary people. They were called the *michimis*. At the very bottom were the slaves. Slaves had been kidnapped from other nations as children, captured in battle, or traded. Most houses had at least one slave. Some families had as many as twelve slaves. In many homes, a person's rank depended on how closely the person was related to the head of the family. It could also be inherited from relatives who died. A person's rank could change through marriage. Because of this, parents usually arranged their children's marriages. Social rankings might also be based on wealth and what a person had accomplished in life.

Family Life

In the Tlingit and Haida nations, people inherited the names, stories, and ceremonies of their mother's family. Members of nations living farther south, such as the Nuu-chah-nulth, could

A Tlingit basket weaver teaches this traditional skill to her young daughter.

decide whether they wanted to be part of their mother's family or their father's.

Children in the Northwest nations were trained in cultural traditions by their elders. The higher the family's rank, the more training the children received. They were taught how to behave properly. They also learned the important songs, dances, and rituals of their house. Through the songs and dances, they learned the history of their family.

Leadership

In most nations, the highest-ranking man in each house was the leader, or chief. A chief was almost always the son of the previous chief. If a leader died, his wife could become the chief. Among the Nuu-chah-nulth and the Makah, the captains of whaling canoes were the highest-ranking people in the community.

The chief made decisions for the house on a daily basis. He also managed food supplies and relationships with other houses. But everybody owned everything together, so all the adults other than slaves could vote to make decisions.

Spiritual Beliefs and Rituals

The Northwest Indians recognized key moments in people's lives with rituals. These moments might include birth, naming, marriage, death, or a change in social status. A family announced and celebrated all important decisions and changes by hosting a ceremony called a potlatch. Potlatches involved several days of feasts and gift giving to the many guests.

Names were very important to Northwest Indians. They were passed down through families. When a person inherited a name from a family member, he or she also inherited that person's social ranking. Children were often given their names at a potlatch. They might get a tattoo or piercing at the same time.

Spiritual leaders were an important part of Northwest Indians' spiritual life. They sang, chanted, and shook sacred rattles to call on the spirit world. They believed harmful spirits could cause physical diseases and spirit sicknesses.

When a girl reached adolescence, she was believed to be in contact with powerful spirits. Often girls of that age had to spend time alone in a small hut made of branches. Close female relatives were allowed to bring her food. The higher the girl's rank, the more time she had to spend alone. At the end of this time, there was usually a celebration.

THE POTLATCH

Northwest Indian culture centered on the potlatch. The word comes from the Nuu-chah-nulth word *patshatl*, which means "sharing." To celebrate an important event, the members of a house invited guests to share in a feast that could last for days. Food such as salmon, seal, venison, and wild berries was served over the course of the potlatch. Whatever was not eaten was taken home by the guests.

The most important part of potlatches was gift giving. The host gave away as many of his family's belongings as he could. Guests received gifts based on their social rankings. Lower-ranking guests might receive a blanket. Higher-ranking ones might receive a canoe or a slave. Copper plaques or shields with engraved designs were known as coppers. These were especially valuable gifts.

The potlatch showed off a host's wealth. Often two rival chiefs would host a competition potlatch. The winner would be the chief who could give away the most. An especially big potlatch brought honor to a family and was remembered for years. A potlatch could leave a family with nothing. But at another family's potlatch, they would regain wealth through the gifts they received.

Men dressed in traditional button blankets, Chilkat blankets, and headdresses prepare to enter a longhouse for a potlatch ceremony.

Vision quests were another important ritual of adolescence. Girls and boys would spend one or more days alone on a mountain. They fasted and prayed to make contact with their guardian spirit being. This spirit being would give them special skills such as hunting, fishing, berry picking, basketmaking, or healing. Each girl or boy was given a personal song and dance too. Throughout their lives, people performed their personal dances and songs during winter ceremonies known as spirit dances. Through the dances and songs, they told stories about their ancestors and the spirit world.

Many nations had secret societies. These are believed to have been started by the Kwakwaka'wakw. The Kwakwaka'wakw had a few secret societies. Their most

These Kwakwaka'wakw dancers wear masks and ceremonial clothing during a winter ceremony.

important society represented violent spirits. They wore elaborate masks and were highly respected. Members of one of the Bella Coola secret societies danced in a four-night winter ceremony. They wore masks representing the spirit of the sun and other spirits of the sky. The dancers acted out their nation's spiritual beliefs.

When somebody died, the family usually disposed of the body quickly. The Tlingit and Haida had several days of mourning before disposing of a dead body. The Tlingit cremated the dead. The Haida put the body in a wooden coffin. The coffin was placed in a grave house behind the main house. The bodies of chiefs or other high-ranking people were cleaned, dressed, and kept for several days. People could then mourn them with songs. Many nations, such as the Tlingit, held memorial potlatches when somebody important in the family died.

CHAPTER 3

CARVERS AND
WEAVERS

The Northwest Indians are famous for their wood carving and weaving. Items used in everyday life were decorated to show a family's social ranking. Northwest Indians also made objects to celebrate family heritage. These objects were used in ceremonies and rituals.

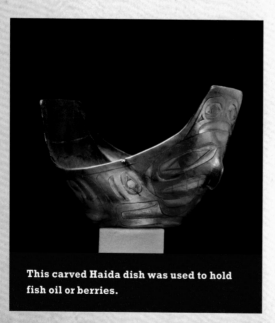

This carved Haida dish was used to hold fish oil or berries.

Wood Carving

The Northwest Indians used wood to make most of their belongings. Some nations, including the Tsimshian and the Chinook, used the horns and bones of mountain goats and sheep too. Northwest Indians made boxes, dishes, spoons, ladles, and fishhooks from cedar. They used tools such as chisels, curved knives, and wedges to hollow

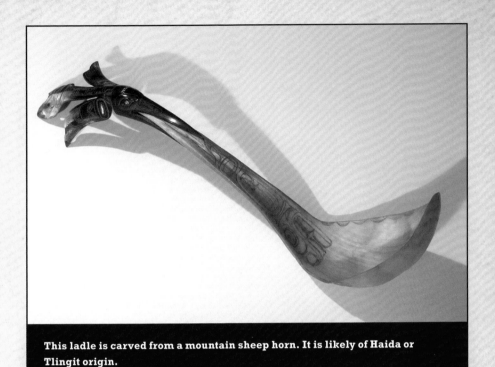

This ladle is carved from a mountain sheep horn. It is likely of Haida or Tlingit origin.

out the wood for dishes. To make a box, they steamed the wood until it became soft. Then they could fold it into the shape of a box. They used sharkskin to sand the wood. They then carved or painted it.

Dishes used at feasts were very detailed. It was important to show a family's social ranking through these dishes. A large feast dish might be the size and shape of a small canoe. Visiting chiefs would eat from it with carved spoons. Guests of lower social status would eat from smaller carved dishes.

Families in most Northwest nations had their own animal symbols, called animal crests. They carved these crests into wooden boxes, bowls, and ladles. One Tlingit serving bowl was shaped like a bear, with shells for teeth. The American Museum of Natural History in New York City has Kwakwaka'wakw dishes shaped like a whale, a sea otter, and a wolf.

Carved ceremonial instruments and masks were important too. Sacred rattles used by spiritual leaders represented fish, birds, other animals, and spirits. They were often lined with abalone shells. It could take years to create a ceremonial mask. Carving and painting them took great skill. The masks might show the spirits of the sea, the forest, or even of an earthquake. Some were

This Bella Coola mask is carved with human features.

creatures such as a whale, an octopus, or an eagle.

Transformation masks were very difficult to make. These masks changed from one face to another when a string was pulled. Many Kwakwaka'wakw myths told of supernatural beings changing into human form. These masks helped tell the story. For example, when closed, a mask could be an eagle. When the string was pulled, two sides flapped open to show the face of a family's ancestor. These masks could be worn by only the members of the family who inherited them.

TOTEM POLES

Northwest Indians are the only American Indians who make totem poles. These poles are usually between 10 and 59 feet (3 and 18 m) high. Totem poles were placed in front of a family's home and faced the sea. Some Coast Salish peoples carved meaningful designs onto the poles that held up their homes instead of making separate totem poles. The poles could be seen from far out on the water. They served as landmarks for those traveling by sea. The Haida and Tsimshian built especially tall poles. They were sometimes more than 100 feet (30 m) high.

Building a totem pole could take from three to nine months. Special care was taken in choosing a cedar tree. Many nations performed a ceremony of gratitude and respect for the tree before it was cut down. Men traditionally carved and painted the poles to show the origins, history, sacred spirits, and animal crests of a family. Some totem poles honored an important person or event. These were called memorial poles. Another type of pole was built on top of a coffin. This was called a mortuary pole. Some nations even built shame poles to point out groups who owed money. Sometimes shame poles are still used to protest a loss of land or an environmental disaster. For example, to protest an oil spill in Alaska in 1989, a Tlingit fisherman carved a shame pole. It still stands in Cordova, Alaska.

These Totem poles, carved with a beaver image *(left)* and an eagle image *(right)*, stand at the Teslin Tlingit Heritage Center in Yukon, Canada.

Weaving

Cedar trees provided material for weaving clothing, blankets, waterproof baskets, raincoats, and hats. Weaving was typically a task for women. They pulled the bark from trees and peeled off the inside layer. They pounded this layer to make it soft and then separated it into thin strands. They used these strands for weaving.

The Tsimshian, Tlingit, and Haida made Chilkat blankets. These blankets involved complex weaving techniques. The Tlingit made especially complex ones. They often took several years of work. Chilkat blankets were made of woven cedar bark strands and mountain goat hair. The bark and hair were dyed and woven into bright designs. The design often represented a family's animal crest. The blankets also had a long, thick fringe.

This Tlingit basket is woven with a killer whale crest.

Owning a Chilkat blanket was a sign of wealth. The blankets were worn as robes for ceremonies and dancing. But usually only a family's chief wore one. If he gave it away at a potlatch, it meant he was especially wealthy.

Northwest Indians also wove baskets. They used baskets for storage and for cooking. Sometimes baskets were used for ceremonies. These baskets might

ART OF THE NORTHWEST NATIONS

NATION	ART
Kwakwaka'wakw	Mask carving
Chinook	Horn carving
Tlingit, Tsimshian, Haida	Chilkat blankets
Haida	Boatbuilding
Coast Salish	Coiled baskets

be decorated with a family crest and show a person's status. To make their baskets, Northwest Indians used the bark and roots of cedar and spruce trees. The baskets were decorated by making patterns in the weaving. They might also be embroidered with colored grasses or painted. Makah baskets were often decorated with scenes of sea life. Other nations decorated baskets with geometric patterns. To create color, Northwest Indians made dyes out of berries or plants. Wild cranberries or sea urchin juice made red. Huckleberries and blueberries made purple. For black, charcoal or mud from sulfur springs might be used.

CHAPTER 4

FORCES OF CHANGE

The Tlingit were the first Northwest Indians to meet **Europeans.** In 1741, Russian explorers traveling by boat arrived in the Northwest. The Russians were seeking sea otters. Sea otter fur was very valuable for making fur coats and robes. The Russians began trading with the Northwest Indians for furs. This trade became very helpful for the Northwest Indians. They got steel blades, knives, cooking pots, cloth, and European clothing.

Soon other European traders arrived. In 1774, Spanish traders landed on the Haida Gwaii islands. In 1778, the British came to Nuu-chah-nulth territory. The newly formed United States also sent ships of traders to the Northwest. The Northwest Indians were already used to trading with one another. They were able to trade well with the Europeans too.

The Chinooks were known as the most experienced and clever traders. They had long been trading with other American Indian nations, especially the Plateau Indians. They had even developed a special language for trading. It was a mix of local languages. It was known as Chinook Jargon or Oregon Trade

Trading posts, like this Hudson's Bay Company post in present-day Vancouver, Washington, became central to trade throughout the Northwest.

Language. When European and American traders came, English and French words became part of this language too.

By the 1820s, the sea otter was almost extinct because of overhunting. European traders began looking for land animals. They traveled north, up the coast. Many Northwest nations, such as the Tsimshian and the Kwakwaka'wakw, traded food and crafts with the newcomers.

But other nations, such as the Haida and the Nuu-chah-nulth, who lived on islands, suffered from the change in the fur trade. Few animals with fur lived on their lands. The Haida were able to keep trading because of their carving and canoe-building skills. But the Nuu-chah-nulth could not continue to trade. European trade disrupted the lives of Northwest peoples. Many communities were left in poverty.

FIRST CONTACT WITH EUROPEANS

DATE	NORTHWEST NATION	EUROPEANS
1741	Tlingit	Russian explorer Alexei Chirikov
1744	Haida	Spanish traders led by Juan José Pérez Hernández
1778	Nuu-chah-nulth	British navigator James Cook
1786	Kwakwaka'wakw	British trader James Strange
1793	Bella Coola	British explorer George Vancouver

The Euro-American traders who came to the Northwest usually treated the Northwest Indians with respect. Most did not settle in the region. The few who did live permanently on the lands of the Northwest Indians knew they needed to have good relations with them. But more and more Euro-Americans began to move to the area. The US government gave plots of land to these Euro-Americans. They moved Northwest Indians from their lands onto reservations. The government forced them to give up their traditions of fishing, hunting, and gathering. Christian missionaries came to teach Euro-American values and

Christianity to the Northwest Indians. The missionaries also took over the education of the children. In Canada, the government outlawed potlatches, saying they were wasteful.

In 1857, gold was discovered in the Fraser River in British Columbia. This brought around thirty thousand people to the region to search for gold. Many came from California, where another gold rush was ending. Euro-Americans invaded Northwest Indian lands throughout British Columbia. Many conflicts broke out between the newcomers and the native peoples.

The discovery of gold in the Fraser River in 1857 brought around thirty thousand Euro-Americans to the region.

The Euro-Americans also brought diseases such as malaria, influenza, scarlet fever, and whooping cough. A smallpox epidemic killed about twenty thousand Northwest Indians along the entire coastline. Among the Nuu-chah-nulth, Kwakwaka'wakw, and Coast Salish nations, one in three people died. Entire communities of Haida were wiped out.

By the late nineteenth century, the Northwest Indians were no longer able to live as earlier generations had. Instead of

Workers pack cans with fish at a salmon cannery in Oregon.

fishing, hunting, and trading, they had to get other jobs. Some became guides for those looking for gold or other mines. Others chopped wood for shipbuilders or worked on farms. When white Americans started canning salmon, the Northwest Indians were able to get jobs because they knew so much about salmon. Some started their own companies in the fishing industry and gave jobs to other Northwest Indians. These Northwest Indians quickly became wealthy again.

As early as 1912, members of some nations in southeastern Alaska formed groups such as the Alaska Native Brotherhood. These groups fought against the way American Indians were treated by the US government. Similar groups formed in British Columbia. They pressured the Canadian government for better treatment. Over the next few decades, these kinds of organizations began to slowly bring about changes in the status and treatment of Northwest Indians.

CHAPTER 5

RECLAIMING RIGHTS

In the late nineteenth century, most Northwest nations were forced to sign treaties that gave almost all of their native lands to the US government. The treaties allowed the nations to continue fishing and hunting on these lands. But few Northwest nations used these rights. New owners of the land often ignored the treaties. They were rarely successfully challenged.

In 1953, Northwest nation leaders formed the Affiliated Tribes of Northwest Indians (ATNI). This organization worked with the US government to establish nations' rights to land and fishing sites. The group fought for health care and the right for nations to govern themselves. It also supported economic development through tourism and other industries. ATNI continues to work to preserve the lands and the cultures of all Northwest Indian nations. But in spite of ATNI's success, some nations, including the Chinook, are still fighting for the rights other nations have achieved. These include health care, education, and the right to have a reservation.

In the 1960s, conflicts over fishing rights began. In Washington, landowners made it nearly impossible for American

Indians to get to the rivers where they usually fished. American Indians who did continue to fish were arrested, and their nets and boats were taken away. So Northwest Indians staged fish-ins on the Nisqually River in protest. The conflict lasted for years. In 1974, a federal judge examined the old treaties. He ruled that American Indian nations could take half the salmon caught each year in Washington's waters.

In 1971, the Alaska Native Claims Settlement returned 44 million acres (17.8 million hectares) and almost $1 billion to Alaska natives. After this settlement, people of the Haida, Tlingit, and Tsimshian nations formed the Sealaska Corporation.

Many Northwest Indians spoke up for their fishing rights on the Nisqually River in 1966.

Sealaska works with businesses that help to preserve the land and its resources. Sealaska also works to preserve the culture of the Northwest Indians.

In 2002, the Potlatch Fund was created by American Indian organizers in Seattle, Washington. This fund seeks to build community through sharing wealth among nations in Washington, Oregon, Idaho, and Montana. The fund supports American Indian education, arts, language preservation, and canoe journeys. The canoe journeys re-create and honor the traditions of the Northwest Indians.

In Canada, Northwest nations also fought to reclaim their lost rights. In 1951, they won back the right to hold potlatches. In 1969, the government of British Columbia started the First Citizens

Canoe journeys have gained popularity in the Northwest Coast as a way for Northwest Indians to honor their traditions and culture.

Haida artist Sondra Simone Segundo demonstrates her unique line of painted footwear during a trade show.

Fund. This fund supports the culture, education, and economy of First Nations peoples. In 1990, the governments of British Columbia and Canada both agreed to begin negotiating a return of land to the Northwest Indians. The BC Treaty Commission was formed in 1992 to oversee the negotiations. Since then, sixty-five indigenous nations in British Columbia have begun working to create treaties with the government. These treaties outline each nation's right to govern itself. They also designate First Nations land. Eight nations have negotiated treaties and are currently putting those treaties into practice.

The Northwest Indians continue to have a thriving artistic culture. Galleries such as Spirit Wrestler Gallery in Vancouver highlight Pacific Northwest Indian artists who create sculptures,

Jim Hart carves a Haida totem pole from an 1,800-pound (816 kg) hunk of cedar.

masks, baskets, and jewelry. Members of Northwest nations still weave Chilkat blankets and carve totem poles. Many nations still hold traditional ceremonies and celebrations. And they teach younger generations about their cultures and languages. One

NORTHWEST POPULATIONS*

NATION	POPULATION
Coast Salish	20,260
Tlingit and Haida	26,080
Kwakwaka'wakw	7,718
Nuu-chah-nulth	7,680
Tsimshian	3,755

*Based on 2010 US and 2014 Canadian data, the most recent available for each region

area in British Columbia began putting up road signs in both English and the Nuu-chah-nulth language in 2016. The peoples of the Northwest also work to preserve natural resources. In March 2016, Canadian prime minister Justin Trudeau met with several First Nations leaders on Coast Salish land. They discussed climate change and how to care for the land. The native peoples of the Northwest are working to protect their land and create a better future for their people.

Kevin Cranmer (Kwakwaka'wakw)

is a carver and a member of the Hamatsa secret society. He carves masks, rattles, and feast dishes. He has also made a 40-foot (12 m) totem pole that stands in Vancouver, British Columbia. For the closing ceremonies of the 1990 Commonwealth Games in Auckland, New Zealand, he carved a 36-foot (11 m) totem pole. His work is on display at the American Museum of Natural History in New York.

Nora Marks Dauenhauer (Tlingit)

works to study and preserve the Tlingit language and stories. Along with her late husband, she published an award-winning four-volume book, *Classics of Tlingit Oral Literature*. Dauenhauer has also published collections of poetry, essays about her life growing up in the Pacific Northwest, and plays that tell traditional Tlingit stories. She has received many awards, including the Alaska Governor's Award for the Arts and the 2005 Community Spirit Award from the First People's Fund.

Deb Foxcroft (Nuu-chah-nulth)

began working as a secretary for the Tseshaht First Nation after she graduated from high school. After nine years, she became the social development coordinator for the fourteen nations of the Nuu-chah-nulth Tribal Council (NTC), focusing on child welfare. She was one of the founding members of an aboriginal child welfare agency in British Columbia. In all her work, her goal has been to change the treatment of aboriginal children in need or at risk.

Charla Lambert (Haida/Tsimshian)

is a scientist who studies how genes control the characteristics of people, animals, and plants. She has degrees from the Massachusetts Institute of Technology (MIT) and the University of Washington. She has also studied at the University of Pennsylvania. She works at the Cold Spring Harbor Laboratory on Long Island, New York. She is a member of the Society for Advancement of Chicanos/Hispanics and Native Americans in Science (SACNAS) and served on the board of directors from 2012 to 2015.

Timeline

Each Northwest Indian culture had its own way of recording history. This timeline is based on the Gregorian calendar, which Europeans brought to North America.

1741 Russian explorers arrive in Tlingit territory.

1774 Spanish traders land on Haida Gwaii.

1778 The British explorer James Cook arrives in Nuu-chah-nulth territory.

1820s Sea otters become nearly extinct due to overhunting.

1840s The US government begins forcing Northwest Indians to move onto reservations and abandon their traditional ways of life.

1857 Gold is discovered in the Fraser River, bringing a flood of Euro-Americans into the region.

1884 The Canadian government outlaws potlatches.

1912 Nations in southeastern Alaska form the Alaska Native Brotherhood.

1951 Nations in Canada win back the right to hold potlatches.

1953 The Affiliated Tribes of Northwest Indians (ATNI) is formed.

1971 The Alaska Native Claims Settlement returns land and money to Northwest nations in that state.

1974 A federal judge rules that twenty-five nations in Washington State have the right to half the salmon caught each year.

1992 The BC Treaty Commission is formed in British Columbia to oversee the negotiation of land claims made by the Northwest Indians.

2002 The Potlatch Fund is established in Washington.

2003 Twenty western Washington nations form the Salmon Defense organization to protect and defend the salmon of the Pacific Northwest.

2015 ATNI leaders hold a summit on climate change. Canadian prime minister Justin Trudeau promises to renew the government's relationship with First Nations peoples.

Glossary

abalone: a type of shellfish that has a shell lined with hard white material, also called mother-of-pearl

aboriginal: relating to people who have lived in a region since its earliest times. In Canada, *aboriginal* refers to the country's first inhabitants.

affiliated: closely connected

artifact: an object made and used by people of the past

cremate: to burn the body of a person who has died

embroider: to sew a design on a piece of cloth

First Nations: the official term in Canada for the nations of aboriginal people

indigenous: descended from the original occupants of a land before the land was taken over by others

mourning: feelings of great sadness after someone has died

negotiation: a discussion in which differing sides try to come to an agreement

preserve: to keep something in its original state or in good condition

reservation: an area of land in the United States specially set aside for American Indians to live on. In Canada, these areas are called reserves.

treaty: an official agreement made between two or more groups

Selected Bibliography

Kent, Susan, ed. *Farmers as Hunters: The Implications of Sedentism.* Cambridge: Cambridge University Press, 1989.

Moulton, Candy. *Everyday Life among the American Indians: 1800–1900.* Cincinnati: Writer's Digest, 2001.

Ostrowitz, Judith. *Privileging the Past: Reconstructing History in Northwest Coast Art.* Seattle: University of Washington Press, 1999.

Reader's Digest Association. *Through Indian Eyes: The Untold Story of Native American Peoples.* Pleasantville, NY: Reader's Digest, 1995.

Renker, Ann M. "The Makah Tribe: People of the Sea and the Forest." University of Washington University Libraries. Accessed January 5, 2016. https://content.lib.washington.edu/aipnw/renker.html.

Further Information

Alaska Kids' Corner
http://alaska.gov/kids/learn/nativeculture.htm
Visit this site to learn about the Tlingit, Haida, and Tsimshian nations as well as nations of the Arctic.

American Museum of Natural History
http://www.amnh.org/exhibitions/permanent-exhibitions/human-origins-and -cultural-halls/Hall-of-Northwest-Coast-Indians
This site has information and detailed photos of objects made and used by eight nations of the Northwest that are on permanent exhibit at the museum in New York City.

Canada's First Peoples
http://firstpeoplesofcanada.com/index.html
This website explores the cultures of the American Indians who lived in the part of North America that is now Canada, including the Northwest Indians.

Gimpel, Diane Marczely. *A Timeline History of Early American Indian Peoples.* Minneapolis: Lerner Publications, 2015.
Learn basic historical facts and important historical dates for five major groups of early Americans, including the Northwest Indians.

Makah Whaling
http://makah.com/makah-tribal-info/whaling
This section of the Makah people's official website describes the nation's important tradition of whaling.

Segundo, Sondra Simone. *Killer Whale Eyes.* Juneau, AK: Sealaska Heritage Institute, 2014.
This book, written and illustrated by a native Haida, tells the story of a young Haida girl with a connection to the ocean.

Index

Photo Acknowledgments

The images in this book are used with the permission of: © iStockphoto.com/Bart Broek (paper background); © Danita Delimont/Alamy, pp. 2–3; © Laura Westlund/Independent Picture Service, pp. 4 (map), 6; © lienkie/123RF.com, p. 4 (tanned hide background); © Todd Bannor/Alamy, p. 8; © George Ostertag/Alamy, pp. 10, 38; © Marilyn Angel Wynn/Nativestock.com, pp. 11, 13, 17, 19, 21; © Eastcott Momatiuk/Stone Sub/Getty Images, p. 15; © Ken Gillespie/First Light/Getty Images, p. 16; © Buyenlarge/Getty Images, p. 22; © Werner Forman/UIG/Getty Images, pp. 24, 26; The Granger Collection, New York, pp. 25, 31; © Robertharding/Alamy, p. 27; © Heritage Image Partnership Ltd/Alamy, p. 28; © Claude Robidoux/All Canada Photos/SuperStock, p. 33; © Archive Photos/Getty Images, p. 34; AP Photo, p. 37; © Marilyn Angel Wynn/Nativestock Pictures/ Corbis, p. 39; © Ricardo DeAratanha/Los Angeles Times/Getty Images, p. 40.

Front cover: © iStockphoto.com/Aimin Tang.